The Dougy Center
The National Center for Grieving Children & Families

After a Murder

A Workbook for Grieving Kids

Cover Art

6-year-old Maggie witnessed the murder of her dad. He was stabbed 13 times.
In her drawing, Maggie transformed her dad's violent stab wounds into 13 butterflies.

Table of Contents

Do You Know Someone Who Was Murdered? 1

What is Murder? 5

Jessica's Story 9

How I Found Out 11

Feelings, So Many Feelings 15

Is the World a Safe Place? 23

Why? 29

Police, Court, and Media 31

Talking to Family and Friends 41

Going Back to School 45

Dreams, Nightmares and Scary Thoughts 47

Remembering: Holidays, Anniversaries and Every Day 51

If Onlys and Wishes 55

Ways to Feel Better: Advice from Kids 59

My Story 63

The End...and the Beginning 67

Do You Know Someone Who Was Murdered?

If you do, you are not alone. Every year, thousands of people are murdered in the United States. That's a lot of people killed. Who are all those people? They are mothers, fathers, brothers, sisters, grandparents, friends. After a murder, many of those left behind are kids like you.

There is a place in Portland, Oregon called The Dougy Center. It is a big house where children, teens and their parents meet together to support each other through the hard times after a death. While they're here, kids like to share their stories, throw pillows, paint pictures and play. Their visits to the center are all about doing things that help with their grief.

Kids at The Dougy Center often tell us how important it is to have safe places to express thoughts and feelings about a death. This book is one of those places. It is *your* book. You can write, draw and color in it, stick things on it, even tear out pages if you like. As you read along, you'll find true stories, thoughts, ideas and advice from other kids who have known someone who was murdered. We hope this book will help you if you don't have a support group to go to, or if you just want to learn more about getting through tough times. Remember, everyone grieves in his or her own way. There is no "right" way to grieve. As you make your way through this book, you may find some activities that you like and others that are not so helpful. Choose what helps and leave the rest.

Before you go on, here are a few tips to help you use this book.
- Keep your book in a safe place.
- Always keep a pencil, pen or crayon handy.
- Keep a stuffed animal nearby. You might feel like hugging it.
- Choose at least one adult you trust who will listen to any thoughts or feelings you want to share as you work through this book.

Look at this book a little bit at a time instead of all at once, if that's easier. Don't worry if what you feel or experience is not the same as what you read about in these pages. As long as you are safe, your way of grieving is what's right for you.

My Photo Album

Use this space to glue or draw pictures of yourself, your family, your friends, or the person who died.

This is a picture of _____

What is Murder?

Until someone in your own family or circle of friends has been murdered, you believe that it is something that happens only to *other* people. People in books, movies or on TV. People in other parts of your city. Perhaps even people on a street or in a park nearby. But not to you. Before the death, you probably heard stories about people who were murdered. Television shows, cartoons, movies and video games all show people or cartoon characters killing and getting killed. No matter how much you may have heard or seen, it is *not* like living through the experience of having a loved one murdered. Not even close. There is nothing in life that prepares you for such a horrible event.

The dictionary says that murder is when a person *kills* another person *on purpose*. Murder is a crime. In a murder, there are killers and victims. The killers are those responsible for the death. The victims are those who die and those who suffer because of the terrible loss. A murder death is violent. Unfortunately, children sometimes witness the death of someone they love. Even if children don't see the murder, they still have a picture in their mind about what happened.

Murders are different from other types of deaths mainly because they are so hard to accept. How do you accept something that is unacceptable? Murder is horrible and wrong. That's what makes it so hard to understand. You may know some facts about what happened. You may find out who the killer is. But there are often many questions that are impossible to answer. Right now, you may have questions about what murder is and what it means. It helps to have someone to talk to about these things. It's important to pick someone who will listen to your questions and answer them truthfully in a way you can understand.

There are lots of different people who might be able to help you. Here is a list to get you started. When you think of someone, write his or her name on the line and circle it.

Parent _____

Grandparent _____

Aunt, Uncle or Cousin _____

Brother or Sister _____

Teacher _____

Friend _____

Counselor _____

Pastor or Rabbi _____

Other _____

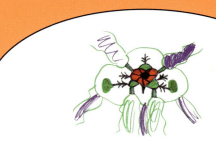

Jessica's Story

Even when you know *what* murder is, it doesn't seem real at first. And, it seems like there is no one else on the planet who has been through what you've been through. Kids at The Dougy Center remember the first time they heard another child tell his or her story about a parent, friend or sibling who was killed. This was the moment they knew they weren't the only one, and they weren't alone. Ten-year-old Jessica's story is about the murder that happened in her family.

> "It was the day before my 8th birthday. My brother Ryan and I just got home from school after a field trip to the zoo. We saw two police cars parked in front of our house. We lived in a brick house on a quiet street. They had put up a strip of yellow tape across our driveway. Some of our neighbors stood on the sidewalk looking at us funny. We were not allowed to go past the tape. When we got off the bus,

"My brother was walking home from work when this drunk man ran him down and just kept going. The people who saw the crash got his license plate number and called the police. They arrested him. I hope he will go to jail for the rest of his life for killing my brother."
—Rodney, 10

"My mom couldn't get hold of our sister so my dad went over to see what was wrong. They found my sister and her boyfriend in a car. They had been killed in a drive-by shooting. We still don't know who killed them. I think some people know but they won't tell."
—Amalia, 8

"my grandpa came up to us. Before I could say, 'What's going on?' Grandpa hugged me very tightly and said, 'We have some very sad news. While you were on the field trip, your dad shot your mom. She is dead.' I looked at my grandpa, and felt confused. How could this be? We were just a regular family. I wanted to go past the yellow tape to see my mom, but the policeman wouldn't let me."
—Jessica, 10

Maybe this story is like yours. Maybe it's different. Now you know the story of two other kids who have had a murder in their family.

How I Found Out

Do you remember where you were when you found out about the death? What time was it? Who told you? Were you there? Many kids say they will remember this moment for the rest of their lives. After a murder, some adults don't tell kids what happened because they want to protect them from the pain. Instead of saying the person was shot, they might tell the child that the person died in an accident. This usually doesn't work for a couple of reasons. First of all, murders are often in the newspapers and on television, so kids find out the story anyway. Also, kids are smart and they figure out things. It's best if adults tell the truth and let kids know exactly what they know. A truthful answer might be "I don't know" because a lot of times, there are no answers. Knowing the truth does not mean you have to know every single detail. But it does mean, at least, knowing *how* the person died. Here are some stories about how kids at The Dougy Center were told about the death, and what that experience was like.

"I don't understand why my mom would do such a thing. It wasn't right for her to shoot my dad. Then why did she have to kill herself and leave us all alone. I just don't understand. My sister tried to get me to go downstairs to see what had happened but I wouldn't go. Then there were police there and they told us that our mom and dad were dead."
—Jade, 9

"When I was three, my sister's boyfriend came into the house and shot her after a big fight. I was in the hall and it was dark and I was real scared. I sat there for a long time 'til my grandma and grandpa came. They told me my sister was dead."
—Mick, 10

Here's what 10-year-old Victor said:

WHO told you?
My mom.

WHERE were you?
At the hospital.

WHEN did you find out?
An hour after my daddy was shot. It was on a weekend.

WHAT happened?
Well, I saw my daddy get shot by a bad man who was trying to rob the store where we were. But Daddy didn't die right away. The police came, and we all rushed to the hospital.

HOW did you react?
I didn't really feel anything at first. I couldn't believe what had happened. Then I felt really, really scared because I thought the bad man would come and get me because I saw him, and he knew I saw him.

Here's what 9-year-old Marlin said:

WHO told you?
A policeman in a blue uniform.

WHERE were you?
In our apartment. I was in the back playing with my action figures.

WHEN did you find out?
It was night. We had just finished our dinner. We had pizza.

WHAT happened?
The doorbell rang, and I ran to answer it. It was a policeman. He asked if he could talk to my dad. My dad came to the door and the policeman said my brother had been stabbed and killed in a fight. I heard my dad make a strange sound in his throat.

HOW did you react?
I was so scared. My stomach hurt.

Who, where, when, what, how?

WHO told you about the death?

WHERE were you?

WHEN did you find out?

WHAT happened?

HOW did you react?

How did you find out about the death? Here is a space for you to write your answers.

Sentence Completion

Example: "I heard Mom screaming and my dad saying, 'oh my God.'"

I saw _____

_____

I heard _____

_____

I smelled _____

_____

I touched _____

_____

I thought _____

_____

Someone said _____

_____

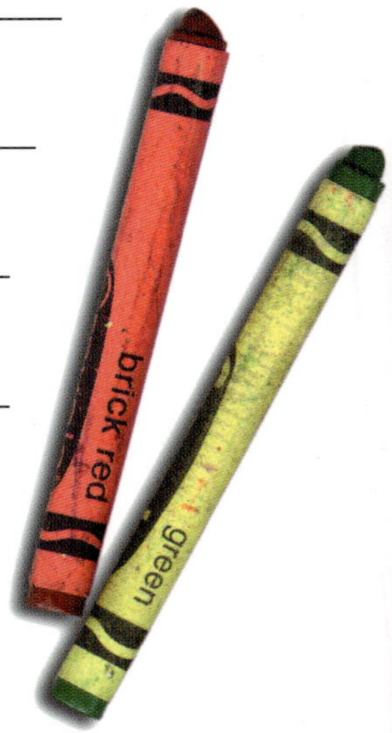

Complete any of these sentences about what you remember.

Feelings, So Many Feelings

Do you remember the story of Jessica and her brother Ryan on page 9? This is Ryan's story. It's about what he felt after the death.

After his mother was murdered by his father, Ryan was numb. "It seemed like all the feelings drained right out of me," he said. "I was like an empty bottle." He walked around in a fog for weeks. The funeral came and went. His aunt asked him why he didn't cry. More time went by. He and his sister Jessica went to live with their grandparents. They changed schools. There was a trial. His father was found guilty and was sentenced to life in prison for killing his mother. There were television stories and newspaper articles. Then, all of a sudden one day, all the activity stopped. People didn't call or come by the house. No one asked any questions or talked about it at all.

"When I make new friends, I don't tell them about the murder. I'm too embarrassed. I think that she'll probably make fun of me and stuff if I tell her. If I get used to her for a little while then I can tell her."
—Chelsey, 7

"I'm angry at my stepdad. He is evil and I wish my mother had not married him or she'd still be alive today."
—Ray, 12

One afternoon, Ryan walked into his room, and looked at a picture of his mom. All of a sudden, he was bombarded by a whole bunch of feelings and thoughts. It was like "a storm hit me," he said. "Like a whole bunch of icy rain kept falling on me stinging me everywhere." At first, he was angry.

Angry at his dad. (How could he DO something like that?)
Angry at God. (How could God let it happen?)
Angry at his mom. (How come she couldn't get away?)
Angry at himself. (How come I couldn't save her?)
He felt like hitting things. He made dents in his desk with his pencil.
He carved his name.

Then he felt sad.
Sad because he missed his mom.
Sad because he could not play on the cool play structure they had in their backyard, and because they sold the pool table in the basement.
Sad because he never got to say goodbye to his mom.

Sad because his family would never be the same.

Sad just because.

Tears came.

The "feeling storms" came and went. There were days when he felt madder than he ever had about anything in his life. It was like a huge swirling thick, dark cloud came and settled over him. Then there were days when the sun poked through the cloud for hours at a time. He played basketball, hung out with his friends and didn't think about it all.

There are many feelings we have when someone dies. It's different for everybody. Sometimes, kids who have had a murder say that their feelings get "put on hold" because of things like the investigation or trial or simply the shock of the experience. It may be weeks or months until they can really grieve. Sometimes, kids don't know what to feel because nobody has told them what is going on.

"I wasn't afraid of spiders and now I am. I saw one on my mom's forehead when she died in her yard when she was killed by her best friend."
—Maggie, 12

"I'm angry at the police because they don't know who killed my sister. They haven't found the person. Until they do, I will always feel this way."
—Cassie, 11

There are no right and wrong ways to feel. It's okay if you cry and okay if you don't cry. You may feel angry or shocked or confused or nothing at all. All feelings are okay. There are some feelings which may seem strange and new after a murder. One of those feelings is rage. It's like anger, but much stronger. You may feel out of control. Or, you might wish to get even with or kill the person who is responsible for the death. That feeling is called revenge.

Strong feelings can be scary and need safe and healthy ways to "get out." Some kids like to talk about their feelings. Some like to do activities when they feel certain ways. Here is a list of some feelings and some activities kids choose when they feel certain ways.

Sad

"Every time I go to my mom's grave it makes me even sadder. I don't know how she died. No one knows. My dad's old friend did it. Now he's no friend at all. People can't be friends if they are going to murder people. I've been through a lot. I fell down and had stitches, and once my eye got scratched, and my chest got two scratches. All that and my mom died too; she was murdered."

—Patrice, 7

Regret

"We were going to go to my grandma's house, and we went fishing instead of going to see her. If we had gotten there, maybe the girl wouldn't have done what she did, and Grandma wouldn't have been lying there in a pool of blood."

—Rebecca, 12

Revenge

"I just wish I could kill the person who shot my dad. I know I won't, but sometimes I have that thought."

—Alessandro, 12

Worried

"Sometimes, if my mom is late getting home from work, I get nervous. I worry that something happened to her too. My stomach gets in knots. I think maybe she'll get shot too. At night I often can't get to sleep because I'm worrying that someone will come into our house and kill us."

—Mason, 8

Relief

"I could have spent the day with her but I decided not to. I decided to go over to my friend's house. And then she left and never came back. She was missing for a little over a year. I thought she had gone away for a while to straighten her life up. And I thought she would come back. When they found her body, I was relieved knowing that I wouldn't have to worry any more about where she was. I knew she was in a safe place. I had just turned ten."

—Kenny, 11

"Sometimes I wonder if there was something I could have done. I used to think that maybe if I'd been a better kid, this wouldn't have happened. I used to bug my dad all the time, so I thought maybe that's why he was drinking and got shot."
—Zoe, 9

Find the Feelings

Here is a word puzzle. How many of these feelings can you find?

Revenge
Afraid
Angry
Confused
Depressed
Guilty
Hate
Lonely
Mad
Sad
Scared
Sorry
Unhappy
Rage

```
H S T D U N H A P P Y R
S C A R E D T G N S H E
P S E U B P L O E R P V
G A N G R Y R Y F A U E
R D A Y F M C E B G T N
A C L O G R A N S E H G
C O N F U S E D P S T E
N U O B I H C L U E E O
R B F I L R H P C T S D
E Y C A T N A F R A I D
S O R R Y G T P E B U I
A E P L O N E L Y L F M
```

Feeling Masks

My Outside Mask

My Inside Mask

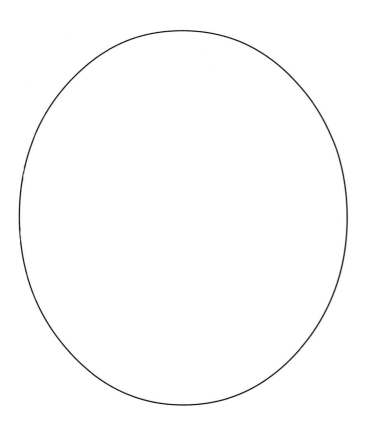

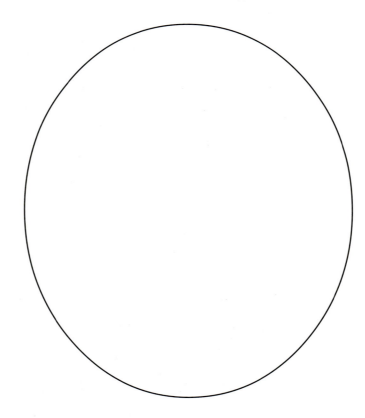

This is how I feel on the outside.

This is how I feel on the inside.

Sometimes how you look on the outside isn't how you feel on the inside. Draw faces on the two masks that show the different kinds of feelings that you have.

"I was afraid the bad man would come and shoot me too, even though he was dead. Then I thought maybe some other scary person would come and get me."
—Eric, 8

Is the World a Safe Place?

After a violent death, kids feel afraid.

A murder is a huge, shocking, scary event that often takes over your thoughts. Imagine if you were watching TV in your living room, and an elephant burst through the front door. It would leave huge muddy footprints, break a lot of things and really scare you. Now imagine a herd of elephants trampling through your living room. You'd be frozen with fear. You'd have nightmares about it. Your family members who weren't home at the time would be scared too because they'd see what a horrible mess the elephants left in their path. In a way, this is what happens in your mind after a murder. Whether or not you were there when the murder occurred, it's hard NOT to imagine what happened and to be afraid it will happen again because of how it impacts everything in your world.

"After my brother was killed at our house by a robber, I would not go anywhere in the house alone. I had to have one of my parents in the room with me."
—Ben, 9

Perhaps the most common fear kids have is that the murderer will come back and harm them or someone else in their family. Even if the murderer has been caught, kids still worry about this. A lot of kids have nightmares about the day the murder happened or about the murder itself. They may be afraid to go to sleep or to sleep by themselves because they worry they will have scary dreams. Sometimes, certain places seem scary because they are reminders of what happened. After her dad was murdered in a park, 8-year-old Misty was afraid to go back to the park, even though it used to be a place where she loved to play.

If you saw a murder, you might feel afraid of anything that reminds you of what you saw or heard. After her brother died in a drive-by shooting, Jasmine was afraid of the sound of cars beeping their horns because that was one of the sounds she heard right after the gun was fired in front of her apartment.

For a while, it might even feel scary to do things you want and like to do. For example, you might find it too hard to think about the good times you had with the person who died because whenever you do, you start to think about what happened. You may want to go to the funeral but are afraid it will make you think about what happened. Just remember, fears are normal. It may take time, but your fears will get smaller. It's important to be able to share your fears with a trusted family member, friend or counselor. Don't hide them. There are practical things an adult can help you do to make your world feel safer. You might just need to hear the voice of an adult or to be held. Some kids like to carry or sleep with an object that makes them feel secure and safe. It may be a big teddy bear, a special toy, a picture of the person who died or a blanket.

Decode the Message

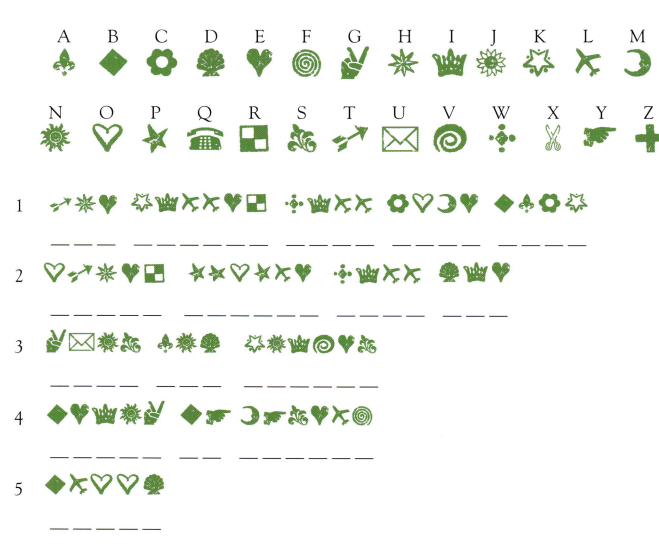

It is normal and natural to feel afraid after a murder. Decode the messages here to learn some different fears that kids have had.

Answers: 1. The killer will come back; 2. Other people will die; 3. Guns and knives; 4. Being by myself; 5. Blood

What Makes Kids Feel Safe?

1. When an adult I trust holds my hand and talks to me.

2. Snuggling with my dog or cat or stuffed animal.

3. Having a night light on.

4. Talking with the police about safety in my neighborhood.

5. Making a safety plan.

6. Knowing the killer is in jail.

7. Having someone else in the room with me.

8. _____

9. _____

10. _____

11. _____

12. _____

Make a list of things that make you feel safe.

Why?

After a murder, people have a lot of questions that are hard to answer. Many start with the word *why*.

Why did this happen to me?

Why won't anyone talk to me?

Why couldn't I stop it?

Why do people kill people?

Why won't anyone tell me what really happened?

You may have asked an adult a "why" question. What did he or she say? What did you think about the answer? Maybe you came up with an answer of your own. Sometimes, there are answers to whys, but often, we have to live without answers. Perhaps the hardest question is, why would someone kill another person *on purpose*?

Here are some answers the kids at The Dougy Center gave. Write in your own answer.

"The guys who shot my stepdad said they did it for 'a thrill.' That is not a reason to kill someone. As far as I know, there is no reason."
—Wade, 14

"My dad could have probably stopped it, by giving the robbers his money. They just thought they had to kill to have it. But they didn't."
—Manuel, 8

"If drugs had never come here, my grandma would have never been murdered. Drugs are killing everybody these days."
—Tyrone, 12

"The man who killed my dad was insane. He had too much hate inside of him that he just lost control of his mind. He was so jealous...and here was a gun in his truck and he decided to use it."
—Logan, 11

_____

_____

_____

Police, Court and Media

Police

The police are involved in every murder. Often, they are the ones who bring the news to a family about the death. Police detectives also work hard to find the killer. When a murder happens, their most important priority is solving the crime. Because of this, they may not be able to let family members get close to the body of the person who died because it is part of a crime scene. Eleven-year-old Dylan remembers that after his older sister was murdered, his mother wanted to put a blanket over her to cover her body, but the police couldn't let her do that.

If a family member is a suspect in the murder, the police may have to question kids and others in the family about what they saw or heard or know. This can be upsetting for everyone involved. They may even arrest a family member and take him or her to jail. In these situations, kids feel like they've lost two people at

"Our dad was a security guard. He was trying to rescue a little boy from this guy who was holding him hostage. He got the boy free but the guy shot our dad. He was killed right there on the street. He is a hero and the police gave us an award for what our dad did."
—Ali, 11

once. Even if a family member is not a suspect, the police may have to question the family or take things from the home which might help provide clues about the murder.

During the time that police detectives are trying to find out who committed the murder, they may not be able to give families information about what they know because it gets in the way of their investigation. This, too, is hard. Families want information so that they can have more understanding and begin to grieve the death. You may have to wait months and years. Sometimes, there is no body found. It is hard to believe the person is dead if you don't see or know that there is a body. Or, you may never learn who the killer is. If a murder case remains unsolved for a long period of time, some families feel like the police don't care about the case anymore.

After a murder, there are safety concerns. One of the helpful things police officers can do is to help your family and your neighbors keep your streets safer or to make a plan for your personal safety.

What are some things the police did that helped? What are some things you wish they had or had not done? Write or draw a picture.

Court

If a person is arrested, there may be a trial. Your parents or caregivers may decide you should not go. Or, you could be required by law to testify at the trial. Either way, it might feel like you didn't have a choice. Another thing that might happen is that your caregivers may not want to share information with you about what's happening. You may have questions that are hard for adults to answer.

Here is Wayne's story:

After Wayne's dad was murdered, the police soon caught the young men who were charged with his death. A trial soon followed. Wayne's mom, Diana, wanted to attend every part of the trial from start to finish. Diana felt that Wayne, who was 8, was too young to be there, and that it would be too hard for him. Wayne's brother, Satchel, had to go to court because he had been with his dad when the murder took place. Satchel, who was 13, had to speak in front of many people about what happened the day his dad was shot.

It was hard for Wayne and Satchel in different ways. Wayne felt left out. To help him feel included, Diana suggested he cut out all the newspaper articles about what happened. This was a good idea, he thought. He pasted the newspaper articles in a memory book he kept of his dad. Each night, he talked to his mom about what had happened that day, and asked her if the reporter had gotten the story right. Diana used many new words he had never heard before. It was confusing at first. But she explained what they meant. Unlike Wayne, Satchel didn't want to be at the trial. He said it was hard remembering the story about what happened. Satchel wasn't much of a talker besides, and especially didn't like talking in front of people. It also made him scared and sad. He worried about the killers. While the trial went on, he went to a counselor who helped him with his fears and worries. At the end of the trial, Satchel felt better because his testimony had made a difference in helping send the killer to prison.

Match the words below to the numbers in the picture. Ask an adult for help if you need to.

____ Charge
____ Jury
____ Lawyer/Attorney
____ Defendant
____ Evidence
____ Witness
____ Verdict
____ Sentence
____ Judge

Murder Trial
This is the event that happens in the courtroom to decide the innocence or guilt of the person who has been arrested and accused of the murder.

Defendant
The person who is accused of the murder. Example: John Smith is the <u>defendant</u> in the trial for the murder of Mary Smith.

Crime
Something someone does that is against the law. Example: The <u>crime</u> that John Smith is accused of is murder.

Charge
The type of crime. Example: The <u>charge</u> against John Smith is murder. Or, another way of saying "accused." Example: John Smith was <u>charged</u> with Mary Smith's murder.

Homicide
Another word for murder. It may happen with a gun or other weapon, or with an automobile.

Victim(s)
The person or people who were murdered or who were hurt as a result of the crime. Example: The murder <u>victim's</u> name is Mary Smith.

Jury
The group of people who listen to a case and decide the guilt or innocence of the person accused of the murder. Example: After listening to both sides, the <u>jury</u> decided that John Smith was guilty of murdering Mary Smith.

Judge
The person who has control of a trial and makes important decisions about cases. Example: The <u>judge</u> decided that John Smith should spend his life in prison for murdering Mary Smith.

Lawyer/Attorney
A person whose job it is to argue one side of the <u>case</u>. "Defense" <u>lawyers</u> argue for the person accused of the murder. "District <u>Attorneys</u>" present information to support the charge made against the defendant.

Evidence
Many different types of information, such as things people say, pictures or objects which are presented in court by the lawyers to support their argument. Example: One piece of <u>evidence</u> the police found was the gun used to commit the murder.

Witness
Someone who speaks about what they saw or what they know about the crime or the people involved. Example: One <u>witness</u> at the trial was Mary Smith's neighbor.

Verdict
The decision the jury makes after hearing the case. Example: The jury delivered a <u>verdict</u> of guilty in the case of John Smith vs. the state of Oregon.

Sentence
The punishment for a crime. Example: John Smith got a <u>sentence</u> of 60 years in prison for the murder of Mary Smith.

Media

A murder is almost always a news story. Whether you want people to know about the death or not, they will more than likely find out in the newspaper, on the radio or on television. Sometimes, you or your family will get a lot of attention and be asked to tell your story by the media. Or, your friends and family may be interviewed. Sometimes, the media will be very interested in a murder trial and will focus on it for a long time. For many kids, who just want to feel accepted and normal, this attention can feel uncomfortable. If the media gets the facts wrong, that can be hard too.

There are positive things the media can do. Sometimes, a news story will focus on special qualities about the person who died or things they did for their family and friends. Kids sometimes hold onto newspaper clippings or videotape as a keepsake. When a story about a murder is in the news, some families find it helpful because it is a way of showing how important it is to keep trying to solve the murder or to prevent it from happening again. What do you think?

Find a newspaper article you liked or didn't like and paste it here. Write one sentence about what you liked or didn't like.

What I liked/didn't like: _____

_____

"My mom's friends would say to her, 'Oh, I'm so sorry,' and then they wouldn't talk to us—the kids. They couldn't handle talking to children about that, and I didn't really like that. If we were old enough to have a parent die, we should be old enough to hear that somebody's sorry about it. And then they would turn to us and say, 'And boy, are you ever getting big!' It made me just get really mad."
—A.J., 11

Talking to Family and Friends

It's hard to talk to people about a murder. Often, people are uncomfortable or shocked or scared when you bring it up. Sometimes, they don't say anything. Or, perhaps they say things that hurt your feelings. When Josiah returned to school after his brother was shot, another boy asked him, "Did your brother do drugs?" Sometimes, kids say things that are just plain silly, such as "I know how you feel because my goldfish died." Usually, it doesn't mean they don't care, but that they are unsure of what to do and say.

Some kids at The Dougy Center say they prefer to choose people they trust with their story. Other kids believe it's important to tell anyone who asks the truth about what happened. You might find that in your family, one person wants to talk openly about the death while others prefer to keep it a secret. You may not have a choice about whether people know or not because it's in the newspaper. Whichever way you choose, remember it's important to have at least one person you trust enough to hear your story.

"Some people think that you are a bad person for not having a dad. Or your dad or your mom was a bad person and that's why he or she was murdered. Some people think that."
—Rene, 10

Telling People

What did you tell people after the murder? What did you choose not to tell them? Write your answers in the bubbles below.

"If your friends are really your friends, They wouldn't talk about it. They would treat you just the same, like there was no murder."
—Jennifer, 12

What I Said

What I Chose Not to Say

The Hurtful and the Helpful

 Say mean things about the person who died.

 Tell me to stop talking or crying about it.

 Ask me if I need help with anything.

 Ask me if I'm doing ok.

 Say they are glad the person is dead.

 Invite me to play.

 Tell me to get over it.

 Listen to me talk about my feelings.

 Give me a nice card.

 Say they are sorry.

 Tell me the person who died must have done something wrong.

Sometimes, the things people do when they find out about a death are helpful. Sometimes they are hurtful. Here is a list of some things people have said or done for kids at The Dougy Center. Fill in a smiling face next to the things below that you think would be helpful and a frowning face next to the ones that would hurt.

Not Wanted   Left Out

"People will start being nicer. Your teachers may treat you different from the other kids. Some kids may be upset and think it isn't fair. Some kids tease you, and some kids will feel sad or not say anything or some kids may not know. I remember what everybody said like, 'I'm so sorry everything happened. If there's anything I can do...,' or 'I'm so sorry. Oh. I'm just so sorry.' Sometimes it felt really good to have attention. But then other kids made me feel bad. It's not your fault your teacher picks you. That's just the way it was."
—David, 9

Going Back to School

In the days and weeks and months after a death, school can be a challenge. When you are grieving, it's hard to concentrate on school work. Some kids may say mean things or do not talk to you at all. Or, your friends and teachers may worry a lot about you when all you want to do is just feel "normal." After a murder, it's also hard to leave home and be apart from people you love. You might be more afraid or feel nervous about things that never made you feel that way before. On the other hand, being at school might feel good because it's a safe place where you can think about other things like friends, projects, activities and subjects you enjoy. You may be fortunate to have teachers and friends who are helpful and understanding. If you are having trouble with your school work, talk with your teacher or counselor about making a plan to help you complete it. Try to get things done just a little bit at a time.

"My teachers always said, 'Do your work, get busy,' because I sat in class and thought about it, and I would get in trouble. If teachers know about the death, they shouldn't do that. They should understand why we're slowing down and not studying. I slowed down a lot. I just sat mostly."
—Brian, 11

School Checklist

Use this checklist to help when you are back in school.

My School Checklist
Name:

Grade:

Date:

Teacher's Name:
With my teacher I will do the following:
- [ ] Talk about any work I missed
- [ ] Talk about work we will be doing
- [ ] Make a plan for doing this school work
- [ ] Talk about taking breaks

My Study Buddy's Name:
My study buddy will help me with:
- [ ] Doing all of my homework
- [ ] Turning my homework in on time.
- [ ] Telling me what my assignments are

The Adult at School I Trust is:
(This person may be a counselor, coach, teacher, nurse, secretary)
This person will help me with:
- [ ] Talking about my feelings
- [ ] Helping me with things I'm scared of or angry with
- [ ] Helping me remember things I need to do

Dreams, Nightmares and Scary Thoughts

Many kids dream about the person who died. Sometimes, dreams are comforting because they help us feel like we have seen, heard, talked to or hugged the person one more time. Nightmares are scary dreams. Sometimes, they can be so frightening that they wake you up, and it's hard to go to sleep afterwards. Some kids have the same nightmare again and again about what happened to the person who died. The images are so awful that they are afraid to go to sleep.

Even in the middle of the day, you may have scary thoughts that pop into your head. It may feel like you can't control the thoughts or make them go away. Some kids have thoughts about what happened or about what the person who died went through.

Dreams, nightmares and scary thoughts are often our brain's way of helping us work things out. Over time, the nightmares usually change, or one day they just stop. The thoughts, which come frequently at first, usually are fewer and fewer. If you have a nightmare, or if you have scary thoughts or pictures that pop into your mind over and over, share them with an adult you trust. Ask the adult to help you find a way to deal with the fear. Here's an example. After his sister died, Nathan had nightmares about attackers. He was also scared of the dark. The first thing he did was to put a night light in his room. Then he built a toy sword out of aluminum foil and cardboard to keep by his bed. He also chose a special bear a friend had given him at the funeral to hold as he fell asleep. He asked his mom to sit by his bed when he went to sleep. After a few weeks, the nightmares went away.

Make a picture or write about a dream or nightmare you had after the person died.

"My brother was funny. He'd take me to my bus stops. Sometimes he might give me candy or go rent a Nintendo game. I used to listen to his tapes. I have his trophies now. They are still his though. They are packed away in the closet. I am so angry that he is gone. And about some other stuff, like probably I'll never see him again. I think of him sometimes. That he might be alive or something like that."
—Felipe, 8

Remembering: Holidays, Anniversaries and Every Day

What do you remember about the person who died? Michelle remembers her mom's laugh, the amazing cherry pie she made and how slow she drove, even on the freeway. Peter remembers his dad's temper and how it sometimes scared him. He also remembers their fishing trips, especially one right before he died when he caught a fish that was bigger than the one his dad caught. Cassie remembers how her sister always promised to teach her to do a cartwheel but then she died before she had the chance.

Memories are important. There are many ways to keep memories alive. One way is to talk about the person. Another is to look at pictures that remind you of special times. Some families choose certain times to honor the person, such as birthdays, the day of his or her death, or holidays. You may also want to plan an activity. Here are some examples.

"My dad was the best horsey. He gave good piggy back rides and he was a good dad. He used to take me where he works, loading Christmas trees, apples and potatoes. He took me on the potato truck. Once I saw all the potatoes being dumped into this truck and that was in Montana."
—Cathy, 7

Remembering the Anniversaries and Other Special Days

Here's a list of special ways to remember the person who was murdered. Circle the ones that you have done, or would like to do. Then write in your own.

Cook a special meal, or treat that they liked

Light a candle

Listen to his/her favorite music

Draw a picture of a special memory with them

Put some flowers on their grave, or in a special place at home

Look through a photo album

_____
Write in Your Own

_____
Write in Your Own

Holidays

Holidays can be especially hard times because we have lots of memories around these times and often we miss the person who died more. Around holidays, some families like to keep traditions they shared with the person, while others prefer to start new ones.

Thanksgiving   Christmas   Hanukkah   July 4

Easter   Halloween   Valentine's Day   Kwanzaa

My holiday _____

What was the favorite holiday of the person who died? Here is a list of a few holidays. Circle one, and write or draw a picture of what you did on that holiday and what you do now. If you don't see your holiday, write it in.

> "My father was just good natured. He kind of had a short temper, but I still loved him a lot. He was really funny and he always got involved in our sports and stuff. Baseball, football, soccer. I just miss him a lot. I don't miss anything in particular. I miss everything about him"
> —Dan, 11

Favorite Activity

Here are two activities to help you remember things about the person who died that make them special. Don't worry if you don't know the answers.

Their Favorite Things

Favorite Food:

Favorite Song:

Favorite Color:

Favorite Animal:

Favorite Activity:

Favorite Place:

Other Favorites:

Things We Liked To Do Together

1.
2.
3.
4.
5.
6.
7.

If Onlys and Wishes

Often after a murder, kids think to themselves, "If only *this* or *that* hadn't happened, the person might still be alive." Other times, they wish the person who died were with them again or that they had told the person something before they died. Sarah, 7, said, "If only my dad hadn't gone out to bars so much before he was murdered, he might not have ended up getting killed in one." Michael, 9, wished he had been able to talk to his mom and tell her he loved her the day she died. It is normal to look back and wonder about what might have happened. Have you ever had thoughts like these?

One thing kids wonder about is what they would say or do if they had the chance to speak to the murderer. What would you say? Some kids find it helpful to write a letter or draw a picture of what they would like to express to the murderer.

"I wish that my friend Joe could come back. And that he was out of all the gang activity. I also wish there were no more gangs because in December another person that I knew got shot."
—Sean, 11

Here's what some kids said they would say or do if they met the murderer face to face.

"I would say nothing. I'm mad at him about so, so much."
—Taylor, 7

"I don't know. I had lots of feelings about him. Bad feelings. I don't want to say. Too offensive to him. Feelings that are really cruel. I have never been able to say those feelings, and I don't want to share them now."
—Janie, 11

"I'd ask him, Why did you kill my mom?"
—Jolene, 11

"I want to find out the answers to all the questions that I have about why he did it. I think he would probably say that he didn't mean it. That it was an accident. And I would think he was lying."
—Berneisha, 12

"You're an idiot."
—Rick, 8

I would say: _____

_____

Kids also think about what they'd say to the person who died if they had just one more chance to talk. Here are a few things Dougy Center kids said.

"'Don't ever leave me again.' And he would say 'I won't'."
—Amanda, 10

"Hi. How are you doing, Bobby? I hope I see you again, Bobby. We miss you."
—Ian, 7

"I would just play, just hold my baby sister. I wouldn't say anything. I don't think she'd understand. Maybe I would say, 'I love you.'"
—Josh, 12

"Hi, Daddy. I love you. Daddy, I miss you. I wish you didn't have to die."
—Briana, 8

"I got to say goodbye to my dad. But I said goodbye because he was dropping us off to our mom. I didn't know it was the last time I was ever going to get to see him. It was cold out and I just hugged him and said, 'See ya next week or two.' I didn't know that I would never see him again. I guess I would just say goodbye."
—Desiree, 13

What Would You Say?

Write or draw what you would like to express to the person who died.

Ways to Feel Better: Advice From Kids Who Have Known Someone Who Was Murdered

Nothing can take away the pain of a death or murder. But the pain does change over time. Things do get easier. And even though there are no "quick fixes" or cures for grief, there are many things kids and families do to help them with their grief and fears. One helpful thing you might already be doing everyday—playing!! Despite what has happened, you are still a kid and kids need and like to play with their favorite toys and games and their friends.

Words of Advice from Kids

Here are ten things kids told us were important during the hard times after a murder.

1. **Don't hide your feelings.**

   "When you hide your feelings, they build up inside you and turn into anger which you take out on someone that is close to you. You're mad about the death but you won't speak about death so you get angry about something else. I've done that a couple of times. But then I just start talking about it."
   —Sara, 15

2. **Don't think you're crazy if you feel bad.**

   "Expect to feel bad and cry a lot. You may feel like you are going crazy because it's like you can't believe they're gone and you will never get to see them again. But you're not. You're just in shock. You're grieving."
   —Lana, 11

3. **Cry…. if you need to.**

   "For me there was a lot of crying. I felt lonely knowing she was gone, and that other loved ones were hurt. But crying always seemed to lift something heavy off me."
   —Ashleigh, 13

4. **Get mad if you need to, and find a safe way to get it out.**

   "You are mad because you have to accept they're gone. I punched a punching bag and screamed into my pillow. Believe it or not, it felt better."
   —Andy, 10

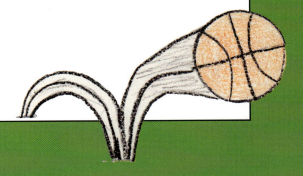

5. **Remember the life of the person who died.**

   "Find a special place to go that reminds you of their life. Keep special things. Keep memories alive. They are all we have."
   —Taryn, 11

6. **Escape for a while in a book, play or a movie.**

   "What really helped me, actually, was books. They took me away. That way I could deal with stuff when I got back. Wherever the books took me, it helped me."
   —Alexis, 12

7. **Do the best you can.**

   "Keep trying to do your best and don't give up. Don't try to get into trouble. Don't blame yourself for what happened. That's what a lot of people do. They suicide or something like that. It's not worth it. Don't give up."
   —Heidi, 12

8. **Find a support group or other people who understand.**

   "My support group took a lot of pain and worries away, just seeing that I wasn't the only one that was going through the kinds of things that I was going through. People were there for me."
   —Billy, 12

9. **Draw, paint, play.**

   "You need to play and forget your troubles and the pain. Part of it you can never get rid of no matter how hard you try. Have fun. Be a kid."
   —Dwight, 11

10. **Know that someday you'll feel better.**

    "I'm starting to be able to cope with it. I mean I think about him every day, but not all day every day. But some days I still think about him."
    —Lauren, 10

Here is a list of things grieving kids do to feel better

- ☐ Write in a journal or draw a picture.
- ☐ Go outside and do something physical, like basketball, running or tag.
- ☐ Play with toys, games or imaginary play.
- ☐ Talk to a friend, adult or counselor.
- ☐ Snuggle with a cuddly toy or blanket.
- ☐ Write a letter to the person who died.
- ☐ Go to a support group for kids who have had a murder death.
- ☐ Take a nap.
- ☐ Punch a punching bag or pound some clay.
- ☐ Cry or scream into a pillow.
- ☐ Laugh.
- ☐ Watch TV with someone.
- ☐ Eat your favorite snack.
- ☐ Say prayers.

My Story

Everyone has a story. Now that you are close to the end of this book, you have read some stories of other kids who have had someone die by murder. Some of them may be like yours and some may be completely different. Now you may want to write your own story. You don't have to write it all at once. You may want to write a little now and add to it later. Or, you may want to draw it. It's up to you.

My Story

Here is a place for you to write or draw your story.

Wave Goodbye

Put your hand in this space and draw a line around it. On each finger write a memory, or what you liked best about the person who died, or what you would say to them if you had been able to say goodbye.

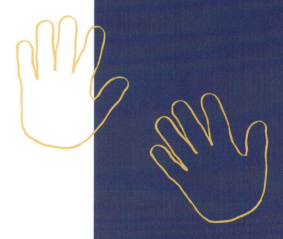

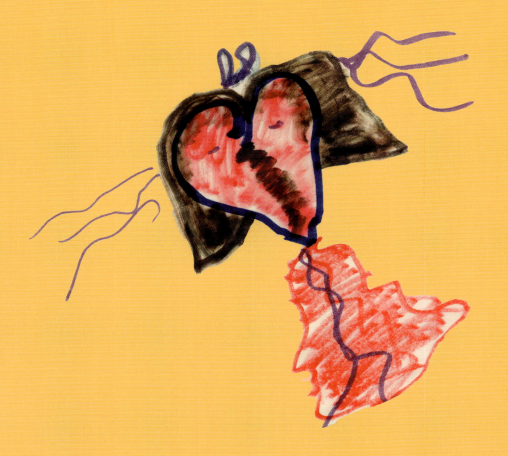

The End...and the Beginning

Even though you've come to the end of this book, you are just beginning a new chapter in your story of grief. Some people say that grief is like a journey. When you started the journey after the murder, you may have noticed that the road was very rough and rocky and it seemed dark. It may still feel that way at times. Now that you've had the chance to hear a little bit from other kids, you know that you are not alone on the road. Other grieving kids walk alongside you. And although the journey of grief doesn't end, the rough parts do get smoother. And often, they sparkle like little lights of hope to help you find your way.

Thank you for reading this book. It is dedicated to you and to grieving kids everywhere.